Those Who Keep Arriving

The Gerald Cable Book Award Series

Those Who Keep Arriving

Julie Danho

Silverfish Review Press
Eugene, Oregon

Cover art: *Le Royaume des Idees* by Carles Piera Claramunt. Art installation. CCCB Museum. Barcelona. Drap Art art festival. 2013.

Artwork used by permission of the artist.

ISBN: 978-1-878851-73-4
Library of Congress Control Number: 2019957441

First Edition
9 8 7 6 5 4 3 2

Published by
Silverfish Review Press
PO Box 3541
Eugene, OR 97403
www.silverfishreviewpress.com

Distributed by
Small Press Distribution
800-869-7553
spd@spdbooks.org
www.spdbooks.org

Printed in the United States of America

Contents

III

IV

For Dave and Elizabeth

Those Who Keep Arriving

I

Erased de Kooning

Robert Rauschenberg wanted to know if unmaking art
could make art. This idea seems too much for me,
having just seen giant irises blooming out of a wall, a painted
lower intestine, a woman's bust sculpted from soap. But I'm standing
before his canvas, his *Erased de Kooning Drawing*, and, like much art,
its title tells me what to see. If you were here, how you would
praise this, how we would argue over whether this was true,
over what, if anything, was. Rauschenberg erased a de Kooning
that de Kooning reluctantly gave him because he appreciated
the idea, and it was, Rauschenberg said, all about the idea.
He erased the painting in celebration, just as you (I wish I could
    believe)
erase me. Not that I'm art, or you're art, but weren't we ideas
of each other? If you were here, you'd make your point, walk away
before you saw that Rauschenberg erased for a month and still
there are ink spots, de Kooning's violet crayon; there are even eyes,
still looking. My love, Rauschenberg lied. The idea,
yes. But how his arms must have ached afterwards.

I Want to Go to Barcelona

as planned, so I can eat tapas at La Boqueria
and look at Picassos and Mirós and a fountain
Calder made of mercury before we knew mercury
harmed the brain and heart. I bought my ticket
after the bombings at the Stade de France,
the massacre at the Bataclan. I picked Spain
over France to feel safer, but that was before
the airport blew in Brussels, and the subway too,
and yes, statistically, the risk is so miniscule
I'm more likely to drown in the tub or get hit by a bus
in Providence, and yes, every day thousands die
in less spectacular ways that we pass over like a jet
above land. But reason isn't what I feel when seeing
cheery photos of the victims, then X-rays of the nails
in their lungs. This fear is a beach ball I hold underwater
as long as I can. Last night my daughter played
in my empty suitcase, pretended it was a plane.

Old Country

The bomb went off in your day,
my night. I wake to deaths
not yours, for the newsman

doesn't say American, doesn't say
woman, and the words not said
are those that let morning begin.

Beirut was just a myth until you left,
a land my Sito fled, then closed
her mouth around. It's different

from the rest, you said, as if
a country small as Connecticut
could ignore its neighbors' knocking,

as if tribal feuds were not interred
in shallow graves, and I had not conspired
with the Maronites, the Shiites,

the PLO, on reasons why
you were wrong to go. When you
threw the ocean over your shoulder,

you vowed to stay a year or two,
just until his visa came through,
and he could wander Midtown

without his crucifix on show. Now,
every Saturday, his relatives sweep you
into weddings at beach resorts,

nights you fold into airplanes
to chiffon across my lawn.
But how can I revel in these brides

who arrive on thrones, or their hired
flame eaters, or their eight-foot
sword-cut cakes, or the seven hundred

shots of arak in their honor, when,
with every dabke, you retreat
further into the dark's full skirt?

They've taught you to smooth
into a leg, a kick, a forward
stomp, those same steps my mother

steps until her wedding film
unspools. My friend, time
runs backward to avoid its end.

It's nearly Valentine's again,
one year since the death of Hariri,
when the streets bared their teeth,

fossilized in the rubble. The protests
you pretended not to attend are over,
and the revolution's ire has grown

as rare as the cedar. But don't tell me
bombs are just for the marked,
for these days only begin that way.

Months from today, you'll ride sidesaddle
to the cathedral, your diamonds blazing
above Romans fallen on Phoenicians,

above Arabs soldered to Ottomans,
their hoary cities all hot for resurrection,
one good detonation. Among these bones

lie maids of old Rome, who gave
their lives as decoys for their brides.
How startled they'd be to find you

in strata of lace and silk, no one to walk
first, no one to hold down the road
that tries to rise as you pass.

Be a Gem

"With just eight ounces of cremated remains and a few thousand dollars, anyone can turn deceased love ones into colorful [diamond] carats." –NBC News

Such a lovely girl, a treasure. What a shame to let her forever
quiver six feet under, when you could keep her here forever.

Gods sob diamonds, said the Greeks. Others put diamonds in mouths
and houses to ward off fevers, liars, phantoms forever.

It's like keeping her curls in a locket, but better. So hold your
     sweetheart
close with a princess cut, and let her rest on your chest forever.

Why not consider another? A ring to celebrate your father, your tragic
baby brother? There'll be enough carbon left—it measures forever.

Meteors harbor diamonds so tiny trillions could frill
the head of a pin. Together, they sequin our forever.

Its powder poisoned sultans and popes. Rebels macheted arms and
     legs
to serve its lure. Diamond always meant "to tame." Later came "forever."

I could lower her, scatter her, wear her as jewels on my wrist.
No matter. Over's over—not one murmur of forever.

It's Terrible What's Happening There

people say, if it comes up I'm Syrian
when my daughter mentions her "Sito"
or I'm microwaving my kibbe at work.
And it is. But I don't need to tell you.
You've heard the numbers of the dead.
You've seen the mothers turned grey.
I never know what to say because I'm Syrian-
American, and I know only as much as you
of the city that bombs are skinning
down to concrete and bone, where children
are sleeping alone in the rubble, where Haddads
and Imondis and Nourys are still living
if they haven't fled or been killed.
When my father's grandparents left Aleppo,
they carried their stories like gold
sewn inside clothes, but no one since
has pulled hard at the stitches. So
my horror is that of a woman who looks
at the sky and expects only blue—a luxury
my ancestors passed down to me.

10% Hope

is what Rothko called for
in his recipe for art. After the war,

the figure dead, rectangles
floated on canvases numbered
instead of named. Hung low,

unframed, they drew us to fields
of whites, reds, violets. As he grew old,

his work grew huge
and dark. He slit his wrists,
and people nodded. Some argue

he sought feeling, others
the sublime. In a brick chapel

in Houston, Texas, fourteen
late paintings stretch
floor to ceiling. Look once,

and they are black.
Again, and they are black

the way the sun is black
when it slowly passes
full behind the moon.

Distance

You can fawn over cancer in a smoker
if you've never taken a drag. You can feel
sorrier when the woman was mugged
late at night. And when a child drowns,
you know you would've latched that fence,
listened for footsteps by the door.
It's said that tragedy draws us closer,
yet we look for a rock to wedge between us
and horror. Today, on the bus route
I take to work, a man stabbed a woman
until she died. It was early afternoon.
I heard it first on the news, and later,
at our stop, how quickly talk leapt
from shock to sympathy to *did she
know him?* Randomness is the mad king
of fear. No one can prepare for the man
who pulls a knife before she even
looks up. The reporter had said,
once it was over, three men held him
until the cops came. Tonight, we waited
in wool and fleece, in down and leather,
in a tight circle of streetlight. Did any of us
wake today and think we'd be dead
by day's end? Maybe she did. After all,
it was her husband, which made us feel
better. It's always safer when someone
is killed by someone they loved.

When the First Father Dies

You're glad it's not your own.
Down the row you say *so sorry so sorry*
and usually for the first you are the sorriest,

for somehow he's deader at 50 or 55
than fathers picked over by time. He dropped clean,
his heart, in the yard. Or cancer,

swum wide and quiet. We know this waits,
rooms tamed by wingchairs, their feet dug in plush.
And once that door's ajar,

you'll be through again, kissing cheek after cheek,
getting down the rhythm of grief: father
before daughter, mother after father

before daughter, if no one misses their cue.
But no matter the soft comforts you utter,
or the number of bodies you hold,

your turn will not be better. Seeing a mugging
isn't being mugged. Holding your breath
isn't a pillow held over your face.

The Betta Fish, Christmas

We have three choices,
he said: kill it, let it die slowly
in the small, cold bowl,
or fork over for a tank
with a heater and filter. The store
had said the half-gallon size
was fine, but not according
to the hours he spent online
after buying this last-minute gift.
Head in his hands, he vowed
not to bring it back in the cup
it had been kept and sold in,
said he'd rather crush it
than watch it suffer, than let
our daughter see it float
dead in days or weeks.
It had been a long, hard year.
Our axis had moved enough
that we could expect land
and step on water instead.
This fish was a tiny red
problem. It barely moved.
We placed the bowl on the desk
as we decided the worth
of its life. Bred for beauty,
the betta would fight another
to the death. But this fish
would not. It would be
only as we said. We looked
at him like a painting
until it came time for bed.

After the Argument

My love, we are electrical animals,
built to be predictable, to hum blood

and oxygen like a continuous tune.
But this doesn't always hold true.

To get the heart back in rhythm,
a surgeon makes keyhole

incisions between the ribs,
threads in camera and catheter

to freeze lesions into the atria's
thin walls. Sixty thousand miles

of vessels, a pump with four wet
mouths: the scars reroute the beat.

Porca Miseria! Chandelier

Sculpture by Ingo Maurer

Dishes don't just break like this—
unscratched, smooth-hipped, looking back
at you. Imagine a woman who does
not throw the china but instead saws it apart
(a plate curve, a split mug, a creamer lip),
sands it down, glues each piece to silver wire,
the wire to a silver pole that holds the bulb
which can't be seen behind such gleaming white.
She hangs it over the dining room table.
It is so lovely she can barely breathe.
When her husband comes home, he'll want
to know if it's a light or a work of art.
It's important, he'll say, to how he feels about it.

II

On Our New House

Statistics say I won't die here
but I will have a baby here, two babies
here, that I won't put them on
a sled and lock them outside here, that I'll
give them hot chocolate, too much
chocolate here, that I'll fight with
my husband here, stay with
my husband here, will drink a bit
too much every so often here,
have sex 2.2 times a week here,
will cook my turkeys dry.
                            Fifty years
he lived here, the man who built
this house. He didn't know,
six daughters in, his wife would go
far before him, that he'd
abandon her garden, let the stove
sit cold. His eldest, reluctantly,
laid down the keys, said, please,
water the blueberry bush, promised
we'd eat fruit big as a fist.

Ode to My Pink Bathroom

How long I've tried to love you, the way
you still blush and gleam like a teenager
in a poodle skirt, unblemished as the day

you were pressed against wire and mortar
in the shower, on the walls, even the floor,
its concrete flecked with pink. The Nolans,

who chose you, are long gone, their daughters
now grandmothers in their own houses,
the blueprints they left behind moldering

in the basement. How can I blame them?
I didn't live through The War, the Boom,
this neighborhood rising up in neat rows

as if each Cape had been pining for sun.
In those years, you were prosperity, pedigree,
First Lady Pink named in honor of Mamie

Eisenhower, her White House bathroom pink
from the walls to the tub to the cotton balls,
so that all over America, millions like me

wake up and stumble into a past that waits
with toothbrush and soap. In you, I saw history
running like a faucet, building to a flood

unless stemmed. But when the contractor
gave me a price, he said you were lead,
and with my daughter...it might be better

to let you be. So I'll own your purr and poison,
though I may dream still of reinvention—
blue trim and *Harbor Grey*—even as I hang

the pink polka dot shower curtain, lay down
that cranberry rug, act as if I chose you,
as if you were everything I ever wanted.

Dear Sito

I hope you're sitting on a gold throne close to Jesus
and are mad as hell at me, clucking your tongue
at how I've become a heathen. I hope Gido's there
to take the fall, that you whisper-hiss in Arabic
how he undid me (*too much TV! all that candy!*)
while he chomps his empty pipe and grins.
You died fast, they said, your heart, in Lucy's driveway,
come to play Tuesday night cards. They buried you
Christmas Eve, and Sito, the poem they asked me
to read…all about Jesus, about your first Christmas
in heaven. There were tears and years and voices
ringing and angels singing and pain in the heart
and we really aren't apart, until the rhyme scheme
burnt up at the end. If you weren't dead, you would've
been proud. You would've loved the good Catholic boy
I married. We gave up Jesus together, the way Gido
kicked cigarettes. Our daughter carries your name,
hangs your ornaments on our tree. That's how
I go on, knowing we won't meet again.

For My Daughter on Her First Birthday

You were late,
but ordinary. Average
height, average weight,

without complication.
When they laid you
on my chest,

you were a frog queen
come up for air,
slick, wrinkled,

your legs splayed
as if ready to leap.
From salt water

and cells,
I formed you
as I was formed,

as your father was
by his mother,
with limbs beginning

as paddles, lungs filling
with fluid. Repetition
should dull wonder,

but you emerged
like a continent
breaking off from Pangaea,

and I held you close,
knowing the ocean
would have its way.

Peanut

First came the itch,
then hives, her nose

doubling, tongue
swelling, throat blocked

like a tunnel suddenly
filled with water.

What a long road
from flower to factory

to the medics rushing in
with syringes, oxygen,

strapping down
that body I forged

in mine, months
sleepwalking through

the universal design
and all its possibilities

for error. Where I find
nutrients, her cells

sense contagion,
commence a nuclear option,

a misunderstanding
spiraling, where

everyone is as innocent
as they are guilty.

How My Father Forgot His Mother

Nine birthdays, Easters, Christmases, nine years
of her pulling on and off his coat and hat,
of spooning his oatmeal into a bowl. I think
she calved off from him like an iceberg

from a glacier, with thundering booms and cracks.
After that, he must have lost her slowly—her name
left unsaid by aunts and cousins who fussed
over his thinness, by the father who butchered

all week in his shop. They meant to spare him,
I'm sure. But she disappeared like ice in the ocean.
Though he remembers days from those nine years,
she's not there. What's left of her is the water

that's risen slowly over decades, waiting for its time
to rush inside, flood room after empty room.

Process Inspiration for the Final Piece

Installation by Carles Piera Claramunt
From *Inner Light: An Art and Therapy Experience at the
End of Life*, Barcelona

More than fifty lightbulbs without light
hang from the gallery ceiling, not from wire
but varying lengths of string, knocking

lightly against our faces, arms, even knees,
no matter how carefully we slip between.
Inside each, in place of the filament,

a feather. The blue-eyed peacock
fills its space like a gas. Others take up less:
the glossy crow shadowing a curve,

the narrow brown and yellow (finch?
sparrow?) straight down the middle,
like a jumper with arms at her sides.

A hundred years ago, this very room
was part of Barcelona's hospital,
where people came to be saved, or try

to be saved, and now we stand here
amidst bulbs with no glow, no heat, useless
except for their glory, the way they bell

off our bodies, their feathers like tongues
either silent or ringing
at a register that's too high to hear.

Early Marriage

In case I catch death's wandering eye,
and my epilogue is but a shriek, a thud,
in case (let's face it), I don't angelify,
or sell you god's lines on undying bonds,

in case what's after isn't back-slap
shivaree, how can I leave so hushed—
our years will age to blip the map
and (cluck the tongue), I'll be the bride of ash.

So young, you won't widow forever:
Another will lie with you all those nights,
then lament over hollows in the bedcover.
Please don't think me sick with foresight;

death isn't what I fear best. It's the living
who must welcome those who keep arriving,
must open their arms to people who keep arriving.

Insomnia

A child, I'd watch the window
for the man with the finger to his lips.

I wanted someone to patrol the night
and now, for months, you stay up

until light, roaming the house
as if dark is both prison and key.

Come morning, you sleep,
a washing machine gone still.

Then night, again, your mind
without brakes

and you asking me
for a tree.

( )

Senator Ted Kennedy (D., Massachusetts) has a glioma brain tumor,
and since we're not far
from Cape Cod (50 miles, if that), local anchors break from weather
and salmonella
(is *your* family safe?) to linger over clips of Teddy when he was lovely
and rehash, for hours, "the curse," as if assassination (at 46) and
assassination (at 42)
and a plane crash (at 38) are the same as getting an old man's cancer.
At 76, the man
has already lived longer than many. After his plane crash (back
broken,
lung punctured) and driving off a bridge (leave it for now), where
another died
and he survived, can we say luck (though lucky would be too much)?

Days past Chappaquiddick, even he (Edward) said *curse* ("whether
some awful curse did
actually hang over all the Kennedys" (*Address to the People of
Massachusetts*, 1969)). After all
he's done (healthcare, gun control, energy policy), the girl sinks
deeper underwater.
We forget how easy it is to forget, when forgetting is easier. (No, my
Gido never left
the scene of a death, but the gambling losing gambling & the passing
it down & the covering it up & me, racing off the bus to him, & him,
cigarillo
housed in his grin, arms flung wide as a Caddy.) No one wants to
believe
it ends like this (the *if only he* laid down to rest).

Sito in the Hospital, 1945

I. American Landscape, 19th Century

Let hill rise and oak sprawl, let the sky
shoulder in. Light still finds her,
four strokes on a wood bench. Her dress
is blue, her head bent. Surely
she hasn't noticed the three small girls
in wide-brim hats. Or, trailing behind,
the man with a long box, his outline
revealed through the cracks.

II. Abstract Expressionism

Half green, half black, a thin white stripe
between. Don't resist the story.
Green for money he took to the track.
Black for her long-dead parents, perhaps
the diagnosis. Anyone would be lost
with three young mouths, empty cupboards,
and a husband who'd sold tales of sugar
and featherbeds. The white is quiet,
the zipper that holds them together.

III. American Portrait, 18th Century

Hair in a tower, she rests one hand
on a weathered table, its feet
in sand. Beyond, the grey Atlantic
is luminous, as is her print housedress,
lead yellow lavished on cotton roses.
Let's call her eyes dull by comparison,
as if worn smooth in the alien sea.
At left, in the corner, hangs a swag
of red curtain, its tassel an arm's reach away.

IV. Cubism

Shattering brings an awkward
beauty. Leg and neck, both there
and here. A prow juts
from a foot. Find the horse's
mane, the fallen cedar branch,
the oud behind her ear. Your mind
will attempt repair. They say
she eloped, abandoned
her country. Find that girl
in this woman, from whom time
slips off like a dress.

V. Pointillism

Approach and watch her disappear.
Step back to make her whole again.
War is in the air, on her hospital gown,
in the blanket at her feet. It is both master
and molecule. His letters beside her
speak only of weather, so she fills in
battlefields dotted with men. Soon,
she will lie next to him again,
and your eyes will blend them as one.

The Museum of Broken Relationships

Of course bears, wedding dresses,
letters for Johns. But also the axe
with butchered bed. The vet's
prosthetic leg. In Sarajevo, Belgrade,
Berlin, they've harbored relics
of soured affairs, sent thousands
touring through loves gone bust:
the Murano glass horse (later
the divorce), the garden gnome
(thrown by the spurned). Here,
you'd think empathy would rise
easy as desire, for who hasn't felt
the ground's cold smack, the ache
of the mornings after? Yet love
folds like laundry, the same story
over and over. The woman who gave
the box made of matches may be
hand in hand with another man.
The man who gave the bowl may
be kneading bread for his new wife.
In the end, there's no marvel
in how we suffer, only in how
we build skyscrapers out of rubble.

III

?

I can't stop lingering
along those curves, the sexy
esoteric way she teeters

on that dot, how she rises
from the basket a cobra
unfazed by my pungi's

charm. A Matisse odalisque,
she teases. No one else
dives with half a parachute,

alights in backless dress.
All I ask is to unhook
that strap, let fabric pool

until it's just her pearl:
small, round, certain
as it's possible to be.

Jenny Perowski Is Ahead of Me in the Grocery Store Line

If an Amish family can forgive the man who burned
their land, surely I can say hello to Jenny Perowski,
who used to call me "fattie fat" in seventh grade math
and had boys call my house, pretending to ask me out.
That was twenty years ago. Now Jenny, if not fat exactly,
is puffy as a slightly overstuffed chair. I'm thinner than her,
and my pleasure feels more whiskey than cream, makes me
want to pour out her Kors bag to rifle for candy, then slowly
eat it in front of her like she once did to me. I know
her cruelty was, at best, a misdemeanor. But anger
is like a peppermint in a pocketbook—everything inside
takes on its smell and taste. I could break it in my teeth,
make it disappear. Instead, I savor the mint, let the sugar
line my mouth like fur, linger far past what can be called
pleasure. How good it would be to be better than this.

My Friend's Breasts

I can't take my eyes off them;
her low round neckline is coy
as a waiter who doesn't ask,
but brings dessert right to the table.
She's telling me about her ex,
but I miss half of what she's saying,
am busy empathizing with men
who can't lift their eyes. This is surely
envy but also marvel—her body
shaped like the letter P, each natural D
pushing off her six-foot frame
like a gymnast in a backward bend.
I haven't seen her in a while, never met
the accountant she caught mid-act.
We're downing rum and Diet Cokes
on a Wednesday at the same Tribeca bar
where we met the last time she was left.
It's silly to expect those breasts,
like the thick rubber on bumper cars,
to keep her unharmed. But I do.
After spending years desiring her
sway over men—they the tourists,
she the mountain terrain—I have to.

Bombshell

Sculpture by E.V. Day

How many men would have fought
to free Marilyn
from that dress?
Someone did,
and left
the dress behind, caught
in a floor-to-ceiling web of fishing line
as hourglass as the actress.   At first
glance, it's lovely, the dress
blown up like the subway
still runs beneath, like hands   still can't resist
the gust.   But the eye loves to rely on memory,
so you'll almost miss   those holes in the billows, the shreds
once tied at the neck,   bits of dress flung   to the web's far corners.
When you find her,
fabric fused to arms and hair,   you'll say get down
but she knows where this is going.

Writing Around the Word

In your letter, not one comma is mis-
placed, not one phrase hangs
midair. Everything is here
but the word. I look up

synonyms—*mishap, mischance,*
meeting with disaster—not one
of which you use. Why,
out of a crowd, did its prefix choose

you, latch onto your hand
as if lost? What is left to bury
but the word? Following your need,
I want to let it fall

back down my throat.
But since I know this grief
thrives in silence, splits
and multiplies until

it presses on your chest
through the night, let me cup
my hands beneath your mouth,
and catch whatever slides out.

Abstraction

On the screen, blacks and whites
expand contract/expand contract,
like mouths trying to force words out.

In this murk, she looks for a body,
comes up empty. I know the possibilities:
it's too early or it never was.

I could hang these images on a wall,
name them *Moon, Clouds,*
Volcano Taken From Above,

and you'd believe each was true.
For years I didn't want to be a mother.
Now need swells like a tick

as she switches on the lights,
then hands me paper towels
to clean off with before I go.

On Deciding to Have a Baby

1.

It's like diving into a lake
the swimmers say is lovely
but looks cloudy and cold—
and you think maybe
they just want company.

2.

To marry, you chose
person, place, time, decided
on fish or chicken. This is
inviting a stranger to dinner
and lifting up your shirt.

3.

Agree to mistrust the facts:
thirty percent less sex,
seventy percent more stress,
that one in five untie the bow
and find an empty box.

4.

A house, two cars, a lump
in the bank, so you wade in
up to your waist, your legs
so numb they almost feel
something like warm.

I Know I'm Saying Like a Lot

by the way he rolls his eyes.
It's like having spinach
in my teeth; I rely on him
to point it out, then cringe
when he does. That little word
veers me into simile—*He was, like,*
veracious—everything turned
comparison instead of stared
in the face. Before him, no one
commented on the litter
in my speech, the kicking
in my sleep, or how my apologies,
like corporate tax law, are full
of loopholes. In theory, I like
honesty, but I hate its metal taste.
He might point out that *He was,*
like, veracious is not actually
a simile, and he'd be right
and I'd be grudging, but
without him, I'm the one
untethered. A month after
our first date, he asked how long
he had to wait before
proposing. He was like
a suitcase, packed and ready.
I felt the same, but never
would've said, never
would've put out my foot
in case there was only air.

O Country

For my blood, I got juice
& a sticker & then sent
on my way. Outside, L Ave

was reeling while businessmen
with Guinness moustaches swayed
in time. Their sloppy brogues turned

heads as they knocked drinks
in the street. When a redhead slipped
me a wink & a beer, I almost yelled

my name like a cheer. This was
my first year as an O'Anyone,
& I hadn't yet tossed the word

back, swallowed it whole, let
it sate my Arabian thirst. Crowds
rushed past as I toasted St. Pat,

let beer flash flood
my senses. Right then, I didn't care
how many snakes remained

in Ireland, how few saints
rolled off my tongue, or that the day
was as American as my love.

When we'd knelt at the altar,
the priest had declared us one,
but history doesn't emigrate

in vows. So I've mapped him
from the outside in, from ocean
to cerebellum, topography

to kidney, every vein checked
& checked again. Now
my blood courses

through a stranger—
accident, operation, anemia—
there's no way to know

why another body took
my O, freely given on a day
when winter played possum

& my head was dizzy
from the blood & the beer
& the years it would take

to never reach what I seek,
to never weary of his pale body
occupying my sheets.

A Long Time Without Touching

After the sculpture *Lot 022405* by Donald Moffett

The card said oil on linen, but that silver
was thick, fibrous, the whole surface
like steel wool unwinding, its long wires
puckering at the center & lifting off
the canvas, thrusting toward me

                            inches & inches of
                            let's get sex out of the way
                            how it strains against itself
                            held back & held out
                            but this might be a fist
                            my eyes are riveted to
                            it was metal I was magnetic he
             applied the paint
with a pastry bag. I had to look it up later
to be convinced. How long did I stand there
waiting for something to happen, waiting
for someone to notice me waiting?

By Which All Things Are Brought Toward Each Other

Gravity is sexy, the way it holds us down,
    lets me walk beside him, roll on sheets
toward him, both of us distant descendents
    of the original matter pressed into fevered
stars, then galaxies—two solid, awkward
    bodies sparking without sparks. I know
little of Newton, less of Le Verrier,
    but nearly two decades in, I'm the Einstein
of him, could fill whole textbooks with formulas
    of our days, as elegant as any that prove
gravity and light travel at the same speed
    or that show if today, suddenly, the sun
disappeared, the Earth would orbit its absence
    for eight minutes—and all that time
I wouldn't know we were adrift.
    How sweet and ordinary that in between
before I discovered everything familiar had left
    as he does, mornings, easing shut the door
so it doesn't make a sound when he goes.

IV

The Night Before Kindergarten

This year, late summer is the time to see Saturn,
so my husband drags the five-foot telescope
to the backyard, fiddles with lenses and charts

as our daughter does somersaults in the dark,
gleeful to be up past eight. I shiver in a T-shirt
and shorts as she lowers her face to the eyepiece,

taking in this planet orbited by dust and rocks of ice,
some large as a school bus, while my husband
explains the rings could be from a dead moon

or what was left over when Saturn was born.
She is impressed, but not as impressed as us
the first time we saw it, when she was weeks old

and we were grateful to be outside where we
couldn't hear her wail, our world grown airless
as a closed jewelry box. To her, the extraordinary

is still ordinary, so why not planets shuttled to the eye
by a tube tall as a sister? We've shut every light
in the house to keep the night clean, to let her see

the show that's all for her, the girl we made
then circled until she knew she was the sun.
Tomorrow we'll send her off to unlearn it,

to discover, as we did, how small we are,
how little we matter anywhere but here.

When the Call Comes

Rise from your desk that is no longer
your desk. Sit in a room designed for this,
windowless, bare except table and chairs.

Your boss reads from a script, instructed
not to look you in the eye, not to apologize,
and he speeds his words until breathing

like an untrained runner. Think not
of your child, your husband, those two
stories of brick and sheetrock saddling up

your back. Take the packet. Resist the urge
to curse or yell or run into the hall
and smash every glassed Monet print,

their lilies dulled by age and light.
The security guard stands still as a wall
as you sit and wait for your boss to gather

your keys, your bag, the things you need
to get home today. The rest will be boxed
and sent. The computers have already

erased you. Upstairs, the day goes on
with hushed words, sympathy teethed
with reasons why it was you. Tell yourself

this is for the best. Maybe now you'll move
from breeze to gale, flute to horn,
from flat road to winding mountain pass.

The Concussion

All the doctor could prescribe was
darkness and quiet: blinds closed,
screens off, no reading, no driving.
I held his arm as he went down
the stairs, walked behind while
he climbed. The snow kept falling,
feet on feet. Water seeped into
the basement for weeks. To be
near him, our daughter multiplied
by book light. Reading, I learned
our brains are softer than the meat
I buy at the market, can be damaged
with just the touch of a thumb.
He never forgot his name, but
could barely sign the medical forms,
the black letters blurring together,
floating like the brain floats
in cerebrospinal fluid, like the embryo
floats in its thin amniotic sac.
How do we rely on these bodies
that are holding tanks for water
and blood? Weeks in, I leaned out
our bedroom window, chopped snow
with a broom until our roof looked
like a smashed sheet cake, its pieces
beginning their slow delicious slide
over the gutter. Had this been any
other winter, he would've waited
with the shovel below. But still
he couldn't tolerate daylight,
and even I had to shield my eyes
from the sun's reflection, wild
and thick with thorns. The doctor
had said a month. It came

and went. Then another. He read
for ten minutes, then twenty.
He started to pull up the blinds
in the morning. How did I feel
the day he walked our daughter
the two blocks to the bus?
Like we'd been fractured,
and our seams filled in with gold.

Easter in the ICU

The body expects rhythm, but this beeping follows
no pattern, each nick of sound refusing to slip
into the background where my aunt and I sit,
making small talk about egg hunts and chocolate
across my uncle's body. We have to fill the space

somehow, and I've already counted the tubes:
the one taped over the hole in his neck,
the one down the throat, the left arm, right arm,
on and on, all labeled with SKUs the nurse comes in
to scan. It's for safety, of course, but odd and cold

and I'm thinking how he'll never again step
in a department store—stroll those long aisles still
competing for his touch. His head is arched back
on the bed, his mouth gaped, like he's trying to hold
his face at the surface while the rest of his body

sinks. My aunt is quiet. Forehead to back,
she strokes his coarse hair flat as these machines,
with each discordant beep, insist *don't sleep*. She
must be the one. They'll make her say it. They make
you say *sleep*, and then they keep the lights on.

On Seeing the Bag of John Lennon's Bloody Clothes

Rock and Roll Hall of Fame, Cleveland

They were in a glass case, in a crumpled paper bag
wrapped in duct tape and plastic, next to a photograph
of his blood-flecked glasses. When Lennon was shot,

I was six, up late with the flu, and my father heard it
from Howard Cosell on Monday Night Football.
He didn't cry or yell, just lowered his head

like my grandfather saying grace, and asked me
to get my mother from the shower. Today,
when we arrived, after hours speeding down I-80,

my parents posed in front of the glass pyramids
like teens on a honeymoon. They led me
to Janis's scarf and her '65 Porsche, to Morrison's

Cub Scout shirt, then let me slip away by the Stones.
That's when I saw his clothes and Yoko's note
about wanting to be shocking. For a moment,

I was rooted. Had she ever dared open the bag
or had those clothes stayed dark and heaped
for decades, made of tougher stuff than the body

they'd been cut off? Somehow it was more of a grave
than a grave, and when my parents came walking
toward me, I steered them away, as if they hadn't seen

more than I, hadn't waited all my life for me
to loosen the strings, even if it wasn't dropping
acid at the Paradise or yelling slogans at cops

in the park. But I've always been more doo-wop
than rock, the Colonial to their tenement.
After Lennon died, there were nights my father

would turn on the stereo and sit on the couch
in his work clothes, still dusty from ripping up
carpets. As the music played, he'd look so distant

that I'd just watch him listen until he asked me
to lift the needle from the record, a moon I'd guide
back to orbit, then hold onto with both hands.

Playing Hide and Seek in the Garden of Heroes

I've never seen it before, this horseshoe of bushes
tucked at the front of the State House lawn,
like a pocket on a wide green shirt. It must be

a secret garden, I say to my daughter, so of course
she races over, and by the time I see those
short flags in the dirt, she's climbing up

the granite marker, pink sneakers muddying
the names of the dead. I pull her off, her limbs
flailing like a beetle on its back. You only

look, I say, and she shrugs, running fingers over
the engraving. She is three. Some of these soldiers
were alive when she was born. There is room left

for more. Come find me, she says, wedging
herself between the marker and the azaleas,
her feet and banged-up knees sticking out

over the gravel path. She is a terrible hider.
I sit on a wooden bench and count backwards
from ten, my eyes open. The slender redbuds

offer no cover, their crowns suited only
for ornament. How wrong it feels to play here,
where people in uniform have mourned.

Some might believe the dead are happy
to see a child keep this garden alive,
but I look over my shoulder for a mother

or father who might see us and remember
playing until everyone was hot and tired.
I pretend not to find her, calling her name

until she laughs and shrieks, runs out
to grab me. I brought her here. For her,
I will hide and hope that no one sees.

Father, 1970

Outside Sip-N-Dip Donuts, he and Drag and Crazy Andy down
    Cuervo until
their blood runs gold, until Charlie lazes by, back enough from
    yesterday's bad acid
to do his Tony Bennett for the troops. He smoothes his storm cloud
    curls,
his torn Doors T-shirt, even sways as he butchers *Put on a Happy Face*
to boos, a beer can clocked at his head. They drink more. Crazy Andy
    seduces
two dozen jellies from the countergirl, and they eat until they're
    powdered white.
Nights, those boys are still there. That lot's so hot they sweat standing
    still—
not one complains. Three are heading over, and my father's number is
coming quick. I know who will die, who will live. I'd never tell.
They're all practicing, and they've got to be ready when it comes.

Cloud Gate, Chicago

*"Nicknamed 'The Bean' because of its shape, this 110-ton elliptical
sculpture is forged of a seamless series of highly polished stainless
steel plates." —NBC News*

Twenty-four people sanded the seams
for months, erasing every line until it seemed
dropped from another place and time, until

it brought down the sky. Sleek, lustered, it steals
the city and returns it softer, more rounded,
pushing the tallest buildings over just enough

so they bow to the rest. We cannot look without
seeing our bodies given back to us, the ground
where we stand commanding as much space

as the sky over this city that burned and rose again,
that learned to move with the wind.
This winter morning, only a few of us wander

in its landscape. Later today, they'll clean
our prints off its surface, so nothing comes
between the city and clouds, so the blue

of its reflection smoothes into the blue of the sky
while the wind roars in like a train.

The Subway Doors Closed

after my husband and daughter
but before me, and she began screaming
on the platform as the train lurched
the length of a few cars, then stopped
hard, the crowd surging forward,
reaching over and in front of me,
trying to force open the doors,
when shouting came from the back:
"Someone's fallen on the tracks!
A child!" I was confused.
My girl had been the only child
on the platform. Panic came on slow
as air bubbles in the water before it
boils but it must have been just milliseconds
before I turned and said, "A child?"
and a woman yelled, "That's her mother!
Get her mother off this train,
this woman needs off the train!"
All went still as they stared at me,
and it felt like the time I flipped
over my car, hitting every side,
then wasn't sure if I was dead
or alive, because I'd been looking
at my child a minute before
and they're saying she's on the tracks
with the rats and the electricity and the trains
charging this way. Had she run toward
the car when it started to move and
slid over the edge? She'd had on
Mary Janes and a polka dot dress.
I pressed myself against the glass,
frantic as a pinned moth, its wings
still beating. I tried to see down
to where she'd been as the crowd

70

murmured like a receiving line,
a few people laying their hands
on my back as, suddenly,
they appeared, my husband waving,
my daughter still screaming.
It was a grown woman who fell.
Not in, but next to, the tracks.
She was drunk, trying to get
the doors open for the rest of us,
so my husband had no idea why
everyone on the train was looking
at the two of them, why people started
hugging and congratulating me
as if she'd just been born.

The Best Chocolate Chip Cookie in New York City

In case there's a line, I show up at seven
but the man at the counter says the cookies
won't be ready until eleven and by then
I'll be on the train, nearly halfway back
to Providence. He and the dozen people
behind me are waiting, so I quickly choose
a ham croissant and a blueberry muffin
glittering like a hotel lobby chandelier.
The shop's a dab of yellow on the block,
its only seats along the front window
where I sit and look at bleary people stopped
at the bodega across the street, touching
apples and mangos until they find the ones
most untouched. With my first bite,
the croissant comes undone, its shawl
falling to the floor. I break off the peak
of the muffin and hear the sugar overfill
the valleys of my back teeth. I'm trying not
to think about how it must taste, the best
chocolate chip cookie in New York City,
how big, how warm, how it would've
collapsed in my mouth, traveled my blood,
made wild pinwheels of my cells.
How much time have I lost
hunting perfection? Once, before cell phones,
before the days when cars couldn't linger
outside the airport doors, my plane was
delayed on the runway for four hours,
and my husband, before he was my husband,
waited for me in his cramped Plymouth
battered from years of lake effect snow.
He just waited, reading a book, turning on
the car every so often to listen to the radio.
When I finally arrived, he was surprised

that I thought he'd be gone. He said
no one asked why he was there so long
or what it was he was waiting for.

Lounging on the Couch on My 39th Birthday in Pink Flannel Donut Pajamas

Surely birds would love to peck
at the dozens of donuts adorning
my arms and legs: the glazed, the jellied,
the vanilla frosted scalloped at the edges
like the worn lace tablecloth in Sito's
tenement apartment where my mother
father sister aunts uncles cousins
would cram in Sundays, post church,
and I'd eat the frosting off two, return
the bottoms to the box while Sito frowned
and Gido insisted I should disfigure
as many donuts as made me happy. After
he died, she pulled the walls around her
like an afghan and didn't leave. Sundays,
when I delivered the church bulletin
to her recliner, she'd clasp my face
in both hands, grateful. It's been decades
since I sat in a pew, but I brought my mother
to the last church hafla, where she won
these pajamas instead of what she wanted
(the platter of walnut baklawa). And maybe
I've lived too long to be lounging in pink
flannel donut pajamas, but I love how they
rub against my legs like a cat's head,
love that someone spent time dreaming up
improbable donuts, like this one here
frosted blue-green, then crosshatched
with piped white stripes, topped with pink
and red sprinkles, a sugared inner tube
floating the middle. How can't I be hungry?
In the next room, my birthday cake sits
on Sito's old table, mine since the day
we emptied her apartment and I opened

dresser drawer after dresser drawer to find
hundreds of crocheted dishcloths, stacked
as neatly as cash for a ransom. We knew
she must have made them in her recliner
by the window on those days none of us
were there. It's almost noon and I'm still
in pajamas, waiting for my daughter
and husband to march into the room
and play me the birthday song they wrote,
her on toy guitar, him on mandolin. I hear
them practicing and it's so sweet my teeth
ache. Sito, was it once like this for you?

I Want to Eat Bugs With You Underground

The scientist on the radio said that humans
will survive, and, at first, I was buoyed,
but she meant only some of us, the ones
living in tunnels, eating crickets to survive
when the rest had died from mass starvation
after droughts lasted longer and seas rose faster
and wars killed bigger because everyone
wanted what little was left. I'd be fine
with being one of the billions dead unless
you were still alive. Under a down comforter
or by a trash fire, I want to be where
you are. You know how poorly I dig holes,
how angry I get when I'm cold, how twice
I've accidentally maced myself, and still
you'd take me with you down into the earth,
give me more than my fair share of caterpillar.
Few believe we're in the middle of the end
because ruin can happen as slowly as plaque
blocking arteries, and only later feels as true
as your hand resting on my hip, both of us
quiet as roses waiting for the bees to arrive.

Acknowledgments

Grateful acknowledgment is made to the editors of the following publications in which these poems first appeared, sometimes in different forms.

Alaska Quarterly Review: "A Long Time Without Touching," "Lounging on the Couch on My 39th Birthday in Pink Flannel Donut Pajamas"

Ascent: "Early Marriage"

Barrow Street: "Be a Gem," "*Bombshell*," "When the Call Comes"

Bennington Review: "I Want to Eat Bugs With You Underground"

Blackbird: "Old Country," "Distance"

Bryant Literary Review: "Father, 1970"

Cream City Review: "On Our New House"

Mid-American Review: "Erased de Kooning"

National Poetry Review: "Abstraction"

New Ohio Review: "Jenny Perowski Is Behind Me in the Grocery Store Line," "Ode to My Pink Bathroom"

Pleiades: "It's Terrible What's Happening There"

Poet Lore: "The Night Before Kindergarten"

Poetry Daily: "Lounging on the Couch on My 39th Birthday in Pink Flannel Donut Pajamas"

Rhino: "After the Argument"

Solstice: "Museum of Broken Relationships"

Spillway: "On Deciding to Have a Baby"

Spoon River Poetry Review: "O Country"

Southeast Review: "*Porca Miseria! Chandelier*"

Southern Humanities Review: "*Cloud Gate*, Chicago," "For My Daughter on Her First Birthday," "When the First Father Dies"

Southern Poetry Review: "Peanut"

Sow's Ear Poetry Review: "How My Father Forgot His Mother"

Sugar House Review: "The Betta Fish, Christmas," "Sito in the Hospital, 1945"

Tar River Poetry Review: "I Want to Go to Barcelona"

Verse Daily: "The Betta Fish, Christmas," "On Our New House"

West Branch: "Writing Around the Word"

Bared anthology: "My Friend's Breasts" (Les Femmes Folles Books, 2017).

Missing Providence, A Frequency Anthology: "Playing Hide and Seek in the Garden of Heroes" (Frequency Writers Project, 2015).

Mourning Sickness: Stories and Poems About Miscarriage, Stillbirth, and Infant Loss: "Writing Around the Word" (OmniArts, LLC, 2008).

Some of these poems appeared in the chapbook *Six Portraits*, which won the 2013 Slapering Hol Chapbook Competition (Slapering Hol Press, 2014).

I am grateful to Rodger Moody for believing in this collection and selecting it for the Gerald Cable Book Award. It is an incredible honor. I also want to thank my writing teachers—Gary Fincke, Bill Roorbach, Lee Martin, and Kathy Fagan—and the editors who published my work, especially Jennifer Franklin and Margo Stever at Slapering Hol Press. Many thanks also to Denise Duhamel for reading this book and for inspiring me with her work.

While drafting these poems, I received the generous support of both the MacColl Johnson Fellowship Fund and the Rhode Island State Council on the Arts. I am so appreciative of the time and resources their fellowships afforded me.

I am lucky to have the work of Carles Piera Claramunt on the cover of this collection. My poem *"Process Inspiration for the Final Piece"* is about his installation that I saw (and loved) in Barcelona, and he could not have been more generous when I contacted him out of the blue.

Many of "those who keep arriving" in this book are my loved ones—they are in these poems both in name and by their influence on my life: my Sito and Gido, my sister Kate Danho, my near-sister Melissa Plourde Khoury, and my parents Carol and John Danho, who have always been my biggest fans and supporters. My daughter Elizabeth makes the most appearances in the book, which feels right. She makes everything better.

More than anyone, I want to thank my husband David O'Connell, an amazing poet, editor, and partner. He appears in some of these poems, but his imprint is on all of them. This book would not be possible without him.

About the Author

Julie Danho's poems have appeared in *New Ohio Review*, *Pleiades*, *Poet Lore*, *Bennington Review*, and *Blackbird*, among other journals and anthologies. Her chapbook, *Six Portraits*, won the 2013 Slapering Hol Press Chapbook Competition, and she has received a MacColl Johnson Fellowship as well as fellowships from the Rhode Island State Council on the Arts. She has a B.A. in English from Susquehanna University and an M.F.A. in creative writing from Ohio State University.

A native Rhode Islander, Julie works as an editor and lives in Providence with her husband, the poet David O'Connell, and their daughter.

www.juliedanho.com

About the Cover Artist

Carles Piera Claramunt is an award-winning sculptor, art director, and producer based in Barcelona. His work uses everyday materials and is heavily influenced by Surrealism, Symbolism, and New French Realism. He has received prestigious awards such as the Drap-Art Emerging Artist Award, the Sant Jordi Fine Arts Award from the Catalan Countries, and Inund'ART 2012. His individual and collective exhibitions have been shown in Milan, France, and Barcelona, among other places. He was the producer of the movie *Tamed Gods: The Origins of Abundance* and was the art director of the movies *Lapin: A Strange Love Story* and *Ànima*.

www.carlespiera.com

@pistonpierart

The interior text and display type were set in Adobe Jenson, a faithful electronic version of the 1470 roman face of Nicolas Jenson. Jenson was a Frenchman employed as the mintmaster at Tours. Legend has it that he was sent to Mainz in 1458 by Charles VII to learn the new art of printing in the shop of Gutenberg, and import it to France. But he never returned, appearing in Venice in 1468; there his first roman types appeared, in his edition of Eusebius. He moved to Rome at the invitation of Pope Sixtus IV, where he died in 1480.

Type historian Daniel Berkeley Updike praises the Jenson Roman for "its readability, its mellowness of form, and the evenness of color in mass." Updike concludes, "Jenson's roman types have been the accepted models for roman letters ever since he made them, and, repeatedly copied in our own day, have never been equalled."

The front cover text was set in Hoefler Titling. An old-style serif font by Jonathan Hoefler, intended as a versatile font that is suitable for body text, it takes cues from a range of classic fonts, such as Garamond and Janson. The back cover text was set in Janson Text, which was designed and cut by the Hungarian punchcutter Miklós Kis in 1685 while he was working in Amsterdam. For many years this typeface was wrongly attributed to Anton Janson, a Dutch punchcutter who worked in Leipzig in the seventeenth century, and the font still erroneously bears his name.

Cover design by Valerie Brewster, Scribe Typography
Text design by Rodger Moody and Connie Kudura, ProtoType
Printed on acid-free paper by McNaughton & Gunn, Inc.